GUN CON
What's the answer?

By
Kenneth Edward Barnes

Contents

Introduction

Why is there such controversy about gun control? One side says, "Guns don't kill people, people kill people." The other side believes that if no one had guns the world would be a much safer place. Who is right? In this little book of about 24,000 words, I look at the argument and see if either side is right and if not what the answer really is. Why am I qualified to write this book? I grew up in the fifties and sixties when the world was much different. Murder was almost not known in the towns and cities where I lived. Now anytime you turn on the local news, there has been a murder, an attempted murder or a robbery. I have also been an author and outdoor writer for many years. I have also owned and used many different types of firearms and have written about them. What I write in this book, however, will probably surprise many that read it.

I know many will jump to the conclusion that since I own guns and have written about them, I will be biased. I can assure you that I will look at both sides and explain the good, the bad and the ugly of the issue. You cannot write about something that you do not know or understand. I have owned, tested, worked on and written about firearms. I have known people that were injured by them and people that were saved by them. Therefore, I will have some surprising insights as to why this is so controversial, what can be done to settle the question, and what the future holds. How do I know what the future holds? Because, I have inside information as to what will happen if either side gets their wish. You may be shocked and surprised at what I am about to say. I am sure that some of what I say will offend a few people from both sides of the argument, but if they really want to know the answer, it will be here. It will be up to each person to look at what I say and then think about it. Many times, when we first hear the truth, it shocks us, or even makes us angry. However, if you really want to know the truth about something you must look for it. And sometimes, it takes a while even after you find it, to understand that it is the correct answer.

During the 1960's the world began to change and not for the better. As a freshman in high school, I remember that one of our teachers had a reloading press in his office. During his free time, he would reload high-powered rifle cartridges he used on his deer hunts out west.

Another time, a classmate brought me a handful of .22 shots shells to take home and try. In addition, as a senior, I could buy .22 cartridges at a local hardware store if the sales clerk called my father and asked if it was all right.

Just a couple of years later, however, things had changed. When I was in the United States army on active duty, I could not buy a box of .22 rimfire ammunition while I was on leave at home! I could not even legally buy a BB cap because I was not twenty-one. My father would have to buy it for me. Why the change?

I was a married man and had a child on the way. I was serving my country during a time of war. Every day I was using an M-16, throwing hand grenades, being trained to fire million-dollar Hawk Missiles at aircraft, yet I could not buy a tiny round of ammunition to shoot at a paper target. This seems ludicrous and was. This is just one thing that happens when people make laws without thinking everything through. This all started for a variety of reasons, which I will explain later.

Recently, I had a review of this book on Amazon. I will let the man's words speak for themselves: ***"I can't recommend this book enough."*** *April 1, 2017.*

"A quick read (that is relative by the way). It is an eye opener, no matter what side of the issue you are on. I started reading with an open mind and just "waiting" for the zinger to happen. The zinger if you can call it that, is to make you THINK. This book makes you think. Please read with an open mind no matter what side you are on. I can't recommend this book enough. (I agree with 99.95% of what is in this book)."

Note: In writing this book, I tried to explain several things in detail so the reader could understand them better. I tried to stay away from being too technical because I did not want to overwhelm the reader with unnecessary information to get my points across. However, in trying to explain certain things, I had to write much more than I wanted, and in doing so, it got very complicated. It soon became apparent that I would've had to write an entire book just to put in all the information. Therefore, I had to simplify much of the information contained in the book. It is therefore written to have enough information to inform those not familiar with firearms without bombarding them with unnecessary details and facts. At the same time, I tried to have enough detailed technical information for those that have a good knowledge of firearms. This way, both sides can better understand what the hoopla is all about and can have a better conversation about the pros and cons of gun control. Because of not putting in too many facts and details, certain topics may be just touched upon or generalized. Most gun owners or those familiar with guns, will readily know what I am saying.

* A BB cap is a tiny .22 cartridge that has no powder inside the case, only priming compound to propel a small round lead ball. It has a muzzle velocity of about 700 feet per second and has about the same power as a good pellet rifle. It is considered a firearm cartridge, however, because it uses an explosive charge to propel the bullet and can be fired in any .22 rimfire firearm, although it can be difficult to load because it is so small. The BB cap was the first self-contained cartridge. It was

invented in the 1840's by taking a percussion cap, putting a rim on it and inserting a small round ball inside. This later lead to the .22 short rimfire cartridge, which was and still is the oldest true self-contained cartridge.

Chapter 1

Knowledge

The first step is to have knowledge about an issue that you wish to discuss or have an opinion on. Today you see people discussing and debating things that they know little or nothing about. They have an opinion, yet they do not know all the facts. This is true in religion, work, politics and many other things.

I may not be the brightest bulb in the lamb, but I have learned a few things in my sixty-five years on this planet. All the time, I see people making mistakes on television programs. I watch movies where they have something out of place, such as an animal that does not belong on that continent or a domestic animal that is supposed to be wild. I watch nature programs and hear them call animals by the wrong name or give out misinformation about them. It takes away from the program because you would think that these people that are supposed to be "experts" would know what they are talking about. I have learned, however, over the years, that you cannot always believe those that are supposed to know. I have also heard "preachers" not telling people the truth, because either they were taught wrong or they just did not read what the Scriptures really said. You would think that when the truth it is right there in black and white, or red and white in some cases, that they would know what they are reading. The same goes for the issue of gun control.

Those that believe a citizen of the United States should be allowed to own and/or carry a gun, argue the gun control issue on one side. They say the Second Amendment to the Constitution gives them that right. They also say they have a right to protect themselves and their families. Others enjoy hunting or target practice.

Some, who are for gun control, want no one to have a gun for any reason, except maybe the police and that may be changing because of all the killing of unarmed people recently. Others just want to keep the flow of illegal guns off the streets. A few want to own a gun themselves, but they think no one else should have that same right. Then there are those in the middle that want stricter gun laws so the wrong people do not get a gun and use it to kill innocent people, as many have done in mass shootings over the last few years.

I will tackle the first hurdle at understanding the issue by those that do not understand firearms. Many are afraid of guns because they do not know one from another or how they work. You cannot discus something if you do not understand the subject. I hear people all the time on television talking about gun control and they have no idea what they are talking about. I will first give a short history lesson as how and why guns are here in the first place. Then I will describe some of the different types and what they are used for and how they work.

Gunpowder is thought to have been invented by the Chinese. No one knows for sure when, but it was probably around 500 to 600 AD. It was first used in celebrations by making fireworks and even small rockets. It was not called gunpowder then because guns were not yet invented.

Many think that sometime during the 1200's gunpowder was used to make a crude cannon. A hollowed-out log with medal bands wrapped around it was supposed to have been the first ones used. A rounded rock was inserted down the muzzle end and it was fired by a hole being drilled above the power charge and lit by a touch or a burning stick.

The next step was to make a cannon from iron and to also use a medal ball. This type of cannon could hold more pressure when fired and therefore shoot farther and hit harder. In the beginning, the breaching of castle walls was usually what the cannons were used for. Later, they were used on ships, mounted on castles walls to protect those inside and some were made to use on the battlefield.

Not long after the cannons were improved, someone had the idea of making a small one that could be held by a man; it was called a hand cannon. It was a small iron tube with a straight rod sticking out the back so that it could be held when fired. This type of weapon could also be used on the battlefield.

The step following the hand cannon was what would be the forerunner of a modern-day gun. The tube that held the projectile was lengthened to look like what we know today as a barrel and a wooden stock was added so the shooter could hold it against his shoulder. By doing so, he could hold it steadier and be more accurate at hitting what he was pointing at. Not long afterwards, someone stuck some crude sights on the barrel to further help in hitting the target.

By the 1500's, firearms were common and were being used in war. They were still crude by today's standards, but they worked. The most difficult problem was how to set off the powder charge that was in the breech. I will not go into all the inventions that were used to make the gun go boom, like the matchlock or wheel lock, but by the 1700's the flintlock came into common use. This was a great step forward and the firearms became much more reliable.

Rifling was invented in the 1500's but was not perfected until 1665 and this was in Europe. Before rifling, the barrels were smooth and accuracy poor. Even after rifling was perfected, rifles were not commonly used, especially in war, until much later. During the American Revolutionary War, most guns used in the battles were muskets, which had no rifling.

As said, the first guns were used for fighting wars. Soon, however, people began using them to take game animals for food or to kill dangerous ones. After firearms became popular and more people had them, competitions were held, either formally or informally. They used their rifles for target practice and turkey shoots. Later, they used shoguns for trap and skeet shooting. Handguns, the first being single–shot muzzle-loading pistols, were also used for target practice, self-defense and even in warfare.

Then, during the 1840's the percussion cap was invented. This was another leap forward.

The next step was the self-contained cartridge, which became popular beginning in the 1860's. After this, the cartridges changed from rimfire to centerfire. By this time, repeating guns were also gaining ground, the 1873 Winchester being one of the first very popular ones.

During the 1880's, the shotgun choke was discovered (inadvertently). This invention gave hunters using shotguns much more range in which to bring down their quarry. Soon after this, 1886, smokeless powder was introduced and we had what is pretty much the modern cartridge of today. It took many years, however, before everyone switched over to smokeless powder.

Minor changes have been taking place for many years, mostly in the design and dimensions of the cases for rifle cartridges and their projectiles or as most call them, bullets. In shotgun shells, there have been many innovations in their construction also, mostly in hulls, wads, and shot. There were many inventions taking place beginning in the mid 1800's, not only in the civilian world, but also in the military. Anyone that has watched a western movie on TV has seen a Gatling gun. A doctor invented it and it is named after him.

During the late 1800's, pump shotguns were brought on the market, and a little later, an auto-loading shotgun and rifle came along. Handguns, too, were being changed. The old single-shot pistols that used flintlock or percussion caps were phased out. During the late 1840's, a man named Samuel Colt came out with a revolver. It used percussion caps and the new revolvers could fire six shots without reloading. It was a giant leap ahead of the old-single shot ones, which were before it. Then, in 1857, Smith and Wesson developed a small tip-up revolver for the new .22 short, metallic cartridge. The previous revolvers used percussion caps, but now a person could just drop the self-contained cartridges into the cylinder and have six quick shots. It was much faster than all the steps needed to load a percussion revolver. This began a revolution in gun designs. The next big step in revolvers was the Peacemaker in 1872, which fired much larger self-contained cartridges. Popular cartridges for it at that time were the 44-40 and the 45 Colt.

When the self-contained cartridges gained popularity, very small single-shot pistols and over-under double-barreled Derringers were often carried for self-defense. Pepperboxes, which were small, multi-barreled guns, were also often used, as was one called a palm gun. A palm gun did not look like a gun, however, for it was round and fit in the palm of a person's hand. The barrel was very short and stuck out between the fingers. It was made for close range self-defense. There were even tiny handguns made for shooting indoors called "parlor pistols".

During the early 1900's, several foreign and domestic companies came out with auto-loading pistols. John Browning invented an auto-loading pistol, which turned out to be one of the most popular guns ever made. It was developed by Colt-Browning, and the year it came out was the name it was called, and that was a Browning 1911.

The differences in handguns are many, but a revolver has a cylinder that holds usually five or six rounds. The number of rounds the cylinder holds is dependent on the caliber and the size of the gun. Therefore, some hold more cartridges than others do. The first revolvers were single-action, which means the hammer must be cocked each time to fire a round. Later, double-actions came along, which means the gun can be fired by just pulling the trigger or it can also be fired by pulling the hammer back as in a single-action. A pistol does not have a cylinder and can be a single-shot or can shoot many rounds if it has a clip to hold the rounds. Many call a revolver a pistol, but it is not. These are the main types of handguns in use today.

Rifles, too, come in single-shot bolt action, multi-shot bolt-action (either clip or magazine), pump or slide-action as some call them, breach barrels or breakdown barrels, or semi-auto. This covers most civilian guns. The military has mostly "assault-type weapons" that can be fired either in the semi-auto or full auto mode. A semi-auto gun must have the trigger pulled for each shot. A "full auto" gun shoots rounds until the trigger is released or until it is empty. It is illegal for civilians to possess or own "fully automatic" guns without a special federal license. Many call semi-auto guns "automatics". They do automatically load the next round after being fired, but they will not keep shooting; the trigger must be pulled each time it loads another round. Some, because of this, call them autoloaders.

Now we come to guns that can cross the line as to what they are. A long gun must have a barrel long enough or it is considered a handgun. A shotgun must have a barrel at least 18-inches long and to cut them any shorter is illegal. With a rifle, it is 16-inches. In addition, both must be at least 26-inches in total length.

When it comes to pistols, things get even more complicated. I will not cover everything but here is something I wanted to point out. You can have a handgun that will shoot a bullet powerful enough to kill a Cape buffalo dead in its tracts, but you cannot have one that will shoot a tiny .410 shot shell without having rifling in the barrel. Some use revolvers or pistols for self-defense that will shoot a .410 shell, but it must have rifling. The companies try to get around this ridiculous rule by having a little bit of rifling at the end of the barrels. I suppose the bureaucrats that came up with this law were thinking it would be too dangerous to have a tiny shotgun. If you are standing ten feet away and are hit dead center with a charge from a pistol that has a .410 shell in it, your chances for survival are slim to none. It does not matter if the barrels are rifled or not. If you are standing one-hundred feet away from the same gun with the .410 shell, and even without rifling, your chances are very good that you will not be seriously injured. On the other hand, if you are one-hundred feet away and are hit dead center with a .357 magnum or a .44 magnum, your chances of survival will be not be very good. This shows that many rounds are far more dangerous and at a much longer distance than a .410 shot shell fired in a pistol or revolver even if they had no rifling. If .410 pistols or revolvers could have smoothbore barrels the range for small game would be increased by only a few yards, but it would be a great survival gun if you were stranded in the wilderness. A much larger shotgun pistol would break your hand anyway. For these reasons, I believe the .410 shot shell handguns should be exempt and be allowed to have smoothbore barrels. The common American gauges are 10, 12, 16, 20, and 28. The .410 is not a gauge, but is the diameter of the bore. If it was called a gauge, it would be a 67-gauge.

In shotguns, there are several types of shells that can be used. Slugs are single projectiles, but most shells have shot in them, ranging in size from large buckshot to tiny shot used for skeet and trap. There are also several kinds of shot. Most are lead, but since lead can poison birds if ingested, several kinds of lead substitutes have been developed, such as steel, bismuth, tungsten-iron and others.

The bullets in rifles are also being changed in some places, such as California, because it can poison the endangered California condor when it ingests bullet fragments by eating dead animals that have been killed by lead bullets. I would think, that in the not too distant future, all lead bullets will be phased out.

Different caliber rifles are used for different kinds of game. The small .22 rimfire is the most popular of all rifle calibers. This is because the guns and cartridges are small, have low noise when fired and are used for small game such as rabbits and squirrels. The cartridges it fires are also the least expensive. This caliber can also be used on somewhat larger animals such as woodchucks, foxes and even coyotes if they are close and the shot is placed correctly. They are illegal, however, to use on big game such as deer. The .22 rimfire is also great for learning how to handle a firearm and many are used for formal and informal target shooting. The rounds are very small but much more powerful than they appear. Therefore, they can be very dangerous if they are used improperly.

Center fire rifles are used on larger game or animals at long distance. Small caliber, center fire guns are used on pests such as coyotes. They are also used for long-range target practice.

Larger center fire rifles are used for big game such as elk, moose, bear, and in the past, for dangerous animals in Africa. They still are used there, but on a much more limited scale due to the fact that poachers have killed off much of the animals that legal hunters used to take.

Shotguns are sometimes used for home defense, but most are used for hunting or trap and skeet shooting. As said, the shotgun ranges from the tiny .410 to the mighty 10-gauge. The smaller ones such as the .410, 28 and 20 gauges are usually used for hunting game birds such as quail and doves. The larger gauges are used for ducks, geese and wild turkeys. The 12-gauge is by far the most popular and is used for everything from quail, to pheasants to deer. Next to the 12 in popularity, is the 20-gauge. It, too, is very versatile and can take most game.

Handguns, too, come in a variety of actions and calibers, from the little .22 rimfire to the massive 500 Smith and Wesson magnum. Small caliber rimfire pistols and revolvers are usually used for target practice and sometimes hunting of small game. The .380 pistols are considered the smallest centerfire personal protection gun that is recommended. However, the .22 rimfire magnum is nearly as powerful. The most popular centerfire caliber is the 9mm auto-loading pistol cartridge and this is what most law enforcement and military personnel use. There are some larger pistols and revolvers used for personal protection or hunting. Most states restrict the use of hunting big game with a handgun that is smaller than a .357 magnum revolver.

I hope this chapter gives you enough information so you will at least know the different kinds of guns, how they work, what they are used for, and their correct names. You cannot argue without knowing what you are talking about or least be taken seriously.

Chapter 2

The Ten Commandments of Gun Safety

I wanted to have this near the beginning of the book. For every year, there are thousands of "accidents" with firearms and even air rifles because those that are using them do not follow safety rules.

I have seen several versions of these rules but they all are similar. Because of not respecting a gun, a tool, or anything that can cause harm, it can lead to injury or death. There are safety rules that need to be followed while driving a car; there are rules when using power tools and the list goes on.

Before I list the rules for gun safety and comment about them, I want to tell a story that happened in my life many years ago. It was around the year 1977 or 1978 and I was home when a friend stopped by for a visit. While he was there, my wife decided to go next door to use the phone. At that time, we had no phone (because of financial reasons) and if we needed to use one, we usually went a quarter mile down the road to my parent's house and used theirs. On this particular day, however, my wife decided she did not want to wait until my friend left so she went next door to use theirs. She also took our two boys, Danny and

David along. Danny, the eldest was about six-years-old and the youngest, David, was about four.

About fifteen or twenty minutes later, as I was in the yard talking with my friend, John, my oldest son, Danny, came running up to me from next door, which was about a stone's throw away. "Daddy," he exclaimed. "David got shot!"

"What!" I said unsure of the news I was hearing. I did not hear a gunshot come from next door; therefore, my first thought was that maybe he was talking about being shot with a BB gun. "What was he shot with?" I asked, "A BB gun?"

"No, a real gun," he answered looking worried.

Now I was scared. "Where did he get shot?" was my first question as terrible thoughts raced through my mind and I could see him lying on the floor dead or dying.

"I think in the leg," he answered.

Looking up, I saw his mother carrying him towards me from next door.

Running to meet her, I felt somewhat relieved when I saw my son looking around; at least I knew he was alive. As I came up beside my wife, I asked where was he shot. "In the leg" she replied and I looked down to see a hole in his upper thigh. David was wearing shorts that day and within five or six seconds, I saw where the bullet had gone in and where it had exited. My worse fear at that moment was that there would be a lot of blood gushing out of the wounds. The holes, however, were clean and the exit wound was not very large. His leg was not broken and even though I was very upset when I saw the wound, I knew he would be okay. I could tell that the bullet had not struck a bone; neither did it hit an artery. I could also tell by the exit wound that it was not an expanding type bullet that he had been shot with.

We still needed to get him to a hospital, however, and as we walked into our yard, my friend John asked what happened.

I quickly explained that he had been shot in the leg and he would be all right but we needed to take him to the hospital. I then asked John if he would mind driving us to there. A minute later, we were on our way.

Anytime there is a shooting, law informant must be called in. Therefore, when we brought my son to the hospital for treatment they notified the county sheriff's office.

David was released after treatment and he was stiff for a couple of weeks, but otherwise fine. I on the other hand, was upset for a longer period of time. It was hard to go to sleep every night and when I did, I would sometimes awaken suddenly and have terrible fear gripping my heart. Therefore, there was not one hour that passed and maybe less, that I did not thank God that my son was not hurt worse or killed.

It took a while to sort out what had happened. There were two men living next door at that time where David was shot. One was about sixty–years-old and his father, who was in his early eighties, was staying with him. The old man used to carry a lot of money around so he also carried a handgun to protect it. He, however, carried it illegally for he had no permit.

On this particular day of the accident, he had tossed his coat on the couch and in the pocket of the coat was a .38 caliber revolver. It was also loaded.

When my wife and boys came in to use the phone, the two men were eating their evening meal. As my wife was busy on the phone, the boys were playing on the couch. I suppose they sat on or moved the coat. Then, either the revolver fell out of the pocket or they found it inside because it was heavy and they were curious as to what it was.

However, they did find it, and from what I know, it was my oldest son, Danny, that came across it first. After finding the gun, my son put it back on the couch and tossed the coat over it. Then, as he had a habit of doing, he jumped backwards onto the couch to sit down. When he did, his hand came down on the coat and the gun under it. His hand must have hit the trigger because this was when it went off. My son, David, was standing in front of the couch, between it and a coal stove. The stove also had a metal shroud around it.

When the sheriff's deputy arrived, we went next door to investigate the scene and he asked the men some questions. On the cushion of the couch, where the gun was lying when it fired, an imprint could easily be seen where the powder burned when the gun went off. The outline of the revolver's cylinder and the barrel's muzzle flash were clearly visible. A few feet away, the shroud around the stove had a large bullet hole in it and a dent was inside on the stove itself. I later put an arrow in the hole of the shroud and lined it up with the large dent the bullet had made on the side of the stove. When I did, the end of the arrow went down at an angle and pointed to the cushion where the gun had gone off. By doing this, it was clear that the gun had been fired as it lay on the cushion of the couch. The entry and exit wounds on my son's leg also showed that the bullet entered low and went up at the same angel before it exited.

Coming back to my house, the deputy and I sat down at our kitchen table and discussed what had happened. My six-year-old son, Danny, was also there to tell what he knew about it.

We knew that the gun had been fired as it was lying on the couch cushion, the problem was; how did the gun get cocked? It was a double-action revolver. This meant it could be fired two ways. One way, was that the trigger had to be pulled and would have to travel far enough to bring the hammer all the way back to fire it. The other way, was that the gun was cocked when it was lying on the cushion. This was the only explanation. The spring that held the hammer back was strong and it was difficult to believe that a six-year-old could cock it.

The deputy sheriff, therefore, unloaded his revolver and asked my son Danny if he could cock the hammer. I do not know how hard he tried, but he was not able to pull the hammer all the way back.

It would be years later, after my sons grew up, that I would know that he did indeed cock the hammer on the revolver that day, but then could not un-cock it. This is why he laid it back on the couch cushion loaded, cocked and ready to fire.

I do not know why my son even touched the gun, let alone cocked it. He had been around guns all his life and knew better. He had never touched or even tried to touch one at home. I had showed him how dangerous a gun could be, but he was a small child and like all kids, he was curious. The responsibility belonged to the man that owned the gun. He should not have carried it illegally. He should not have had a loaded gun on the couch when there were children in the house.

I was lucky that day, as were my two sons. When they used to fight, I would sometimes tell the oldest that he should not fight with his little brother. I said that he was very lucky to still have David with him, because he could have easily lost him that day.

This is another reason I am writing this book. If people followed the rules about handling a gun, there would almost never be an "accident" with a firearm.

I have seen more than one version of these "The Ten Commandments of firearm safety", but they all are very similar.

Here is the first: Always treat a gun as if it is loaded. This is where so many "accidents" happen. "I didn't know the gun was loaded!" If they would have just followed this first simple rule, the accident would not have happened. Each type of firearm is a little different. You need to be familiar with each and every one that you touch. I have seen movies where they say things like, "The gun can't fire if the magazine is removed." This is a lie! If a round is already in the chamber, it is ready to fire, just as soon as it is cocked, the safety is off, or the trigger is pulled; it just depends on the kind of action the gun has.

If you handle a gun, point it in a safe direction and make sure it is empty. Open the action and look into the chamber. This is the *only way* you can be sure that the gun is empty. A truly empty gun is no more dangerous that a lead pipe.

The second rule is to never point a gun at anything or anyone that you do not intend to shoot. Always keep the muzzle of the gun pointed in a safe direction. I'm sure you've hear this, "I was cleaning the gun and it went off accidently." They just broke the first two commandments. They did not make sure the gun was unloaded and they did not keep the muzzle pointed in a safe direction. If they had, that accident would not have happened.

The third one is to never load or cock the gun unless you are ready to shoot. Now this can depend on the circumstances. I have an owner's manual from one gun manufacturer and this is what they have in the book: *Warning*: "Failure to secure a firearm may result in injury or death." Now, right below it, they say this: *Warning*: "Securing a firearm may inhibit access to it in a defense situation and may result in injury or death."

Normally you do not have a loaded gun in the house and the ammunition is stored in a secure place. This is true especially if you have small children. Some children are more trustworthy than others are, but they are all curious. They also might have friends over that do not know anything about a firearm. This is another reason that many gun accidents occur.

I have always lived in the country and many times, I have had grab my rifle in a hurry to take care of pests that were trying to kill my poultry, such as raccoons or opossums. Because of this, I kept some rounds in the magazine of the gun, but never in the chamber. This way, the action of the gun would have to be opened and closed, and then the safety would have to be taken off to fire it.

In addition, if there are not any children around and you have a firearm for home defense, it needs to be loaded and ready to grab in a hurry if there is any danger. All guns manufactured today have some type of safety. If they do not have a safety, they must be cocked to fire. Semi-auto handguns have a clip and you can either have the clip in or out. Even with the clip in and loaded, the chamber can be empty. This is usually the preferred way to keep or carry them. When you are ready to fire, the slide is pulled back, thus loading and cocking the gun.

There is one other thing I should mention. You cannot always count on a safety to work. Once while I was testing a new rifle, I put the safety on and pulled the trigger to test it. The gun fired! Evidently, there was grit or some foreign matter around or under the safety button. The type of safety on this particular rifle was a pin that went behind the trigger, which kept the trigger from moving back. The foreign material prevented the safety to completely engage, which allowed the trigger to still move back and fire the gun. The safety appeared to be on, but was not. Since this was a new gun, the grit probably got in it at the factory. This is the only time this has ever happened. I did point the gun in a safe direction, even though the safety was on, when I pulled the trigger. This is the reason you always keep the muzzle of a gun away from anything that you do not want to shoot. This also goes to show that any mechanical device can fail to function properly, even new ones. Often it takes many rounds fired through a new gun to get it operating smoothly.

The fourth rule is to always be sure of your target before you fire at it. This is often why there are hunting accidents. Someone saw movement and fired at it without knowing what they were shooting at. This should never be done. Most sportsmen and sportswomen know the game laws and if they shoot the wrong animal, or sometimes even the wrong sex, they can be in for a big fine, gun confiscation and even hunting privileges taken away.

When I was in high school, I had a friend I sat beside in one of my classes. We often talked about deer hunting and other outdoor pastimes. He was the boy that brought me a few of the .22 shot shells to try that I mentioned at the beginning of the book.

While deer hunting one weekend with his younger brother, this young man was involved in a hunting "accident." He was sitting in a ditch, watching a field for a buck deer that might come his way. As he sat there, he needed to use his handkerchief. As he took the white handkerchief from his back pocket and brought it around to his face, he suddenly heard a blast from a 12-gauge shotgun. The shotgun was loaded with a giant lead slug that weighed nearly an ounce and had about 2,000 foot-pounds of energy as it left the barrel. The slug struck my friend in the jaw and shattered the bones and several of his teeth. His younger brother, without making sure of his target, had shot him. Only buck deer were legal game and he did not identify that it was even a deer, let alone a legal buck. When he saw the flash of the white handkerchief, he thought it was a deer's tail going up. If he would have followed the rules this "accident" would have never happened. His brother did live and when he finally came back to school, he told me how it all had happened. A hunter not only needs to identify the animal before he shoots, he also needs to place his shot in a vital area so the animal will be cleanly killed. If he cares for the animal, he does not want to wound it or let it suffer a long death.

I also had a great uncle that was squirrel hunting once who had a close encounter. He was sitting on the ground, behind a log, under a nut tree waiting for a squirrel. After a while of sitting there, he thought he would try to call a squirrel by making the barking sound of one. After giving the sound, he suddenly heard the blast of a nearby shotgun as the cap he was wearing flew off his head.

Another squirrel hunter had heard a "squirrel barking" and seeing something brown on the log move, thought the cap was a legal target. The swarm of shot went right over the log hitting the hat without touching my great uncle's head beneath it. He kept the hat for years showing it to people and telling the story. This is just another example of someone not making sure of their target before shooting.

I myself was squirrel hunting once and saw, out the corner of my eye, a squirrel jump from the ground to the base of a hickory tree. I watched the tree for a minute or so and suddenly a camouflaged hunter stepped out from behind it. The "squirrel" I had seen jump onto the tree had been the man's boot move as he took a step. He was behind the tree; therefore, I only saw the movement of his boot.

When I was about twelve, an older neighbor boy, Donald and his friend were squirrel hunting when they found a squirrel hiding in a tree. Donald was going to make the squirrel run while his friend shot it. However, in the excitement of watching for a running squirrel, the friend had the rifle he was using, cocked and pointed towards Donald. Then he happened to touch the trigger and the gun discharged striking Donald in the lower back. Donald was very lucky that his friend was using a low-powered .22 short in the rifle and not using a more powerful round or a shotgun. The bullet missed any bones and did not penetrate deep enough to hit any organs. The bullet lodged in his back muscle where is still to this day.

In addition, when you are aiming at a target, make sure no one is near to the line of fire and know what lies behind the target. Some bullets can travel a very long way.

Most can remember several years ago, when Vice-President Chaney accidently shot a fellow hunter while he was quail hunting. The man was also lucky that he was not real close and the shotgun Chaney was using was a small 28-gauge, which had a light load of tiny shot.

You need to also understand that bullets can ricochet; therefore, you should never shoot at a hard surface or the surface of water with a rifle. In some states, as it is in Indiana, it is illegal to shoot the surface of water unless you are in the legal pursuit of wild game.

As teenagers, my friend John and I were target practicing one day near the Ohio River when John found an old crochet ball that had floated up in the flood waters. It was several feet away when he first saw it and thinking it would make a good target he mounted his .22 rimfire rifle and took aim. When he shot, however, the 29-grain lead bullet hit the wooden ball and bounced back. Lucky, John was standing between the rock-hard target and me. The bullet hit him in the side, near his hip. It did not break the skin, but it did leave a noticeable bruise. I learned a valuable lesson that day and I am sure that John did, too.

It sounds as if there are a lot of accidents with guns. Most, however, are caused by carelessness or being unfamiliar with them. I lived on a state highway for many years and saw several deaths from auto accidents. There were usually at least two or three bad wrecks per year. One terrible accident involved a car full of kids, where three of the children died, plus the driver. In nearly every case, the wreck was caused by a drunk driver. Just as with driving a car, always remember that alcohol and guns do not mix.

The next rule of gun safety is to never climb or jump anything with a loaded gun. This should be obvious, but many accidental shootings to the person carrying the gun happen this way. I once had an uncle that was not climbing, but going through a fence with a loaded single-shot shotgun. He did leave the gun on the other side of the fence, but then he pulled the gun through it. As he did, he pulled it through muzzle first, the exposed hammer then caught on the barbed wired, pulled the hammer back and it fired. Luckily, the charge of shot went between his body and arm. He should have unloaded it or never pulled the gun toward himself with the muzzle end. He broke two commandments and that nearly cost him his life. Another person that I heard about had a similar accident and he was not so lucky. As he went through the fence, he was struck by the blast. He lived, but no longer could claim that he was complete man, as the shot took away his manhood!

Another rule is to always make sure that the barrel is not obstructed. This means do not let the muzzle ever touch the dirt or mud. If the barrel does touch the ground, make sure it is clear before it is fired. I once took my young cousin out shooting and he jammed the end of his shotgun barrel in the mud and did not check it. Luckily, I saw it before he or anyone else fired it.

In addition, if the gun has been stored a while, check to make sure that nothing has clogged up the barrel. Small mud dabbers have been known to build their nests in gun barrels (and also in my duck call). Even a lizard or other creepy crawly things could find a gun barrel inviting. Any obstruction could cause the gun barrel or chamber to rupture when fired and could kill, blind or injure the shooter or bystanders. In loading a gun, also make sure you have the correct ammunition. The wrong ammo can cause catastrophic results. This is especially true if a smaller gauge shotgun shell is loaded into a larger gauge and goes down the barrel where it becomes lodged. Then, if another shell, the correct one, is inserted and fired, both will go off, causing the barrel and maybe the chamber to explode in the shooter's face. This cannot only injure or kill the shooter, but any bystanders.

This brings us to the next safety rule. Always wear ear and eye protection when shooting or even standing close to a shooter. In my younger days, this was not common practice. Because of this, my hearing is not very good in my left hear. This is bad, because I have had a hearing loss in my right ear since I was a child.

Lastly, be respectful of other's property. This means do not shoot at things that should not be shot at, such as roadside signs or anything belonging to others. Everyone has seen signs along the highway with bullet holes. Often behind these signs are homes. The idiot that shot them broke two more commandments. Shooting at signs or power lines and such is illegal. People that do this, gives other gun owners a bad reputation.

It sounds as if guns hurt a lot of people by accident. In nearly every case, it is because of carelessness and not following the rules. Other things also cause many accidents. I know two men that lost a finger or the tip of a finger in a lawn mower. A little three-year-old boy, that lived a few miles from me, drowned in a ditch just a while back. Everyday people are injured or killed in countless ways, sometimes by their carelessness and sometimes by other's carelessness.

Gun safety should be taught to every child. In fact, everyone should know and understand how different guns work and how to safely handle one. In our pioneer days, nearly every man, woman and child on the frontier needed to know how to use a gun. A child is curious and if they happen to come across a gun, they are very likely to try to play with it. If they understand the dangers and are familiar with how they work, it could also lessen the risk of an accident and cause them to stay away or keep others away from the danger.

Today there is so much over reaction because of the gun violence and other violence at schools that there have been knee-jerk policies put in place. Some of these policies are completely stupid. I have heard of some schools that have a "zero tolerance" for anything that might be seen as "a threat". I heard of one little girl that was expelled from school because she came from parade practice one day with the "wooden gun" she had used, which she stored in the trunk of her car.

There was another story, and I knew the boys personally because they were my two youngest sons. At that time, they were living with their mother in a distant city. After school one day, they were playing in the schoolyard and found a "toy gun" someone had thrown away in the bushes.

When one of them recognized that it was a toy (I had taught them to know the difference), he picked it up and was looking at it. Just then, a teacher happened to look out the window and saw him with it. Both were immediately expelled from school. Later, when there was a hearing, it was discovered that they had not brought the toy to school, but had found it as they said. It did not matter, however, for they had "zero tolerance" for anyone that would have "a gun" on school property. I think in cases such as this, the people of the city should have "zero tolerance" for adults in authority being so stupid and they should be the ones kicked out of school permanently. That teacher and the school should also be very proud of themselves. For now, my son that found the toy gun, can no longer walk, talk, see out of his right eye well, or use his hands properly, because of a disease that struck him down when he was only twenty-four-years-old. When he got sick, he did not have a good job because he did not have his high school diploma. Because of having no money, he also had no health insurance or enough money for treatment. If he would have graduated, maybe he would have. He also has three little children.

Chapter 3

Military or Civilian?

As said before, when our country was founded, the guns used for hunting, home defense and military warfare where the same. Nearly all the guns were muskets because rifling would not be widely used until the next century. Each part of the gun was also handmade. Therefore, if something broke, the piece had to be made again. It would be many years before mass produced products would be on the market.

It was not until after the Civil War that guns used in the military were different from those used by civilians. In fact, many civilians had better guns than the military. During the Civil War, a repeating rifle was produced that was loaded by inserting bullets into the butt stock. Abraham Lincoln actually fired one out behind the White House. He thought this type of gun would help end the war sooner. In addition, towards the end of the war, a lever action, repeating rifle made its appearance; it was the Henry.

These repeating rifles cost quite a bit, therefore the army could not afford to buy very many. During the Indian Wars, the army's choice of weapon was a single-shot rifle. This was one reason Colonel

Custer and his men did not last very long at the battle at the Little Bighorn. Many of the Native Americans had repeating rifles, while the soldiers only had the single-shot rifles.

By the First World War (the so-called war to end all wars), our military's general issue gun was a bolt-action repeating rifle. This type of rifle would be the standard issue weapon until the Vietnam "Conflict." Machineguns were used during World War I and World War II, but the rifles carried by the majority of soldiers were still the bolt-action rifles.

Some, during the Second World War, used the "Tommy gun." This little, fully automatic rifle was the forerunner of the standard issue military guns now used. A small semi-auto M1 Carbine was adopted by the United States military in 1941 and was also used during the Second World War.

When I was in the Army, in 1971, the rifles used by most soldiers was the M-16. This is the type of rifle that many now call "assault weapons'. It was a lightweight semi-auto or full auto as it had a selector switch so it could be fired either way. It fired a slightly modified .223 cartridge, which was called a 5.56 mm cartridge. Up until this type of gun was popular, the military guns and many civilian guns were basically the same. The usual differences in military and civilian guns were that the military ones were built tougher to withstand the rigors and harsh conditions of war. The actions, however, were more or less the same. The facts are, from the founding of our country until the invention of machineguns, the guns used by civilians and the military were nearly the same. Semi-auto guns have been around for more than a hundred years. After World War II, they became more popular. The men coming home from the service were used to them and liked the low recoil and rapid fire.

Today, people label guns as being "assault weapons" only because they look different and look like the ones used by the military. In reality, they have been around for a long time, just the outside has changed.

Chapter 4

The Second Amendment

"A well-regulated militia, being necessary to the security of a free state, the right of the people to keep and bear arms shall not be infringed." This is the Second Amendment to the Constitution of the United States. This amendment was written shortly after the Revolutionary War. The first 10 amendments were proposed on September 25, 1789. They were ratified on December 15, 1791.

The reason this second amendment was added was because the states did not want Congress to be able to disarm them. In the late 1700's, the weapons used to defend an individual or to fight in a war where the same. Most used long guns without rifling, because rifling was not widely used. Rifles were also a disadvantage on the battlefield because it took longer to load them. The propellant was black powder, and the guns were muzzleloaders that used flintlock mechanisms to fire them. There were other weapons as well. Single-shot pistols and shotguns, even a few people still used a blunderbuss.

The militias were mostly civilian-soldiers that could quickly grab their trusty muzzle-loading guns and rush to fight if need be. There were some trained military personal but most militia at that time were part-time. The army relied heavily on the ordinary men of cities, towns and farms to come to the aid of the state or country if they were needed. Most of the militia only wanted to fight if the fighting was close by so as to protect their families and property.

This was the way the country was when this amendment was written. This amendment was written so the state would be "secure" and "free." Why would a state need to be secure and free? Secure from what? Free from what? "A well-regulated militia" was made up of ordinary men of the state that knew they could be called upon to fight. Who or what would they be called on to fight? Besides the local Native Americans that sometimes wanted the new comers to leave and never come back, there was the threat of a foreign country invading. The other reason was threats from another state or even the federal government. The states were afraid that Congress could take away all weapons and leave the states defenseless. The states had rights and were to be free from the federal government.

This is why the Second Amendment was created. "The right of "THE PEOPLE" to KEEP and BEAR arms SHALL NOT BE INFRINGED." That is what the Second Amendment says. It says that it is a RIGHT for the people to KEEP and BEAR ARMS..." That means to have them at home or in their possession. The last part says,

"SHALL NOT BE INFRINGED." Bear means to carry on the person and infringed means to restrict that *right*. Laws, however, have done just that. If the ones in authority can do away with the Constitution, which they have on numerous occasions, then anything can happen. The Constitution says, WE THE PEOPLE. It does not say "We the city leaders"; it does not say, "We the governor"; it does not say, "We the Congress"; it does not even say "We the Supreme Court."

The Supreme Court has made decisions that have caused untold grief. A handful of judges deciding what the Constitution says for millions and millions of people. Sometimes even a child can see how stupid their decisions have been.

Chapter 5

Night of Decisions

This is a story that is in my books, *Barnestorming the Outdoors* and *Outdoor Adventures with Kenny*. Most of the stories in those books are about hunting, fishing, nature and conservation. This story, however, is different from all the others and I felt it should be included in this book.

It was on a lonely, rural back road nearly two miles from the nearest human dwelling where this story took place. On this same gravel road, several years later, an armed man with a semi-automatic weapon hid in some bushes and waited for a truck and its three passengers to come by. When they passed, he riddled their truck and the occupants full of bullets.

My story takes place only a few hundred feet or so from the very spot where this incident was to later to place. My friend John and I were scouting different strip mine pits late that spring evening to listen for bullfrogs. Frog season would soon be opening and we wanted to find some good places to hunt them.

Turning off the gravel road onto the dirt road that led back to the pit that night, it was very dark. For some reason before I left home that evening, I had grabbed my single-action .22 caliber revolver to take along I had a permit to carry it, but I rarely took it anywhere except when hunting or target practicing.

Going back to the pit, John pulled up to the water's edge, parked, then turned off the engine. He had removed the top from the International Scout just that day so we were now sitting under the stars.

A few minutes later, the frogs began their nightly chorus, with their bellowing calls, breaking the silence of the quiet evening. One particular frog sounded huge.

"This sounds good," I said. "That one sounds really big."

John agreed and we sat listening for a few more minutes until we thought we probably heard all the frogs that were there. We would come back in John's pick-up truck when frog season opened and bring the boat and trolling motor so we could cruise around the edge of the water and gig or shoot the large green amphibians.

Starting the engine, John began heading back out to the gravel road. The dirt road we were on was the only way out and bordering the road was a large drainage ditch on one side and the water from the pit on the other.

Going a couple hundred feet or so, we suddenly saw something in our headlights. It was a man and he just stepped out of the bushes beside the road. What was shocking, however, was that he had a high-powered lever-action rifle in his hands.

Walking to the center of the road, he stopped and faced us with the gun in front of him. We had not seen or heard any vehicle anywhere when we arrived at the pit or all the time we were there.

Fear suddenly gripped my heart as if a giant hand had squeezed it. Then before I could analyze the situation, another armed man stepped out to join the first. They both now stood in the center of the road blocking our only exit.

My heart raced. I had never been in a situation such as this before. Questions flooded my mind. Why were they here in the middle of nowhere? Why were they armed? Why didn't we see or hear a vehicle? I could only come to one conclusion; they meant us harm! I could literally see newspaper headlines in my mind: **TWO MEN FOUND SHOT TO DEATH, ROBBED AND THEIR VEHICLE STOLEN**. I could see our cold lifeless bodies lying in the ditch beside the road.

What do I do?" I thought.

Then a determination came over me. I have to stay calm. My straight thinking might save my life and John's.

Taking the loaded revolver in both my hands, I cocked back the hammer and held the gun between my knees.

Looking over at John in the darkness I softly spoke, "If something happens, floor it."

John nodded. This was all the time we had to discuss anything. I only hoped he knew what I meant.

Nearing the two men, John slowed down and stopped a few feet in front of them. The men then walked around to John's side of the open Scout. I held the revolver tightly; ready to take action in a split second.

"What's the trouble?" John asked.

I could hear the nervousness in his voice. He was counting on me if things went wrong. There were two of them with high-powered rifles and one of me with a not-so-powerful six-shooter, a single-action that must be cocked before each shot. However, I had had a lot of practice. Once while hunting for mushrooms, a large, black rat snake was in my path that I didn't see. As I neared, it suddenly began rattling its tail in the leaves, which made a sound like a rattlesnake. Then before I even could think, I had my revolver drawn, cocked and pointed, ready to fire.

The action with the snake was pure instinct because I had no time to think before I acted. In this case, however, I had to do everything by thinking about it beforehand. This night, however, I did have one advantage. The men did not know that I was armed. They could not see in the darkness that I held the loaded, cocked gun between my knees.

One of the men then spoke, "We got our truck hung up."

"Sounds reasonable," I thought, "but why didn't we hear or see anything?"

Then they asked a strange question, "Could you take us to the shop?"

"The shop," I thought.

John and I had grown up here. This was literally our backyard. We knew of no "shop." It didn't make much sense; and still, why were they armed? Why did they block the road with rifles in front of them so we could clearly see their weapons?

"Where's it at?" asked John.

"Just up the road," the other man said.

My mind raced trying to figure out what they could mean. Was it just a ploy?

They then began going around to the back of the vehicle to get in even before John had said yes or no.

"Are the guns loaded?" John asked as they climbed in behind us.

"Don't worry," one said, "we won't shoot you," but he laughed when he said it, which did not ease my mind. The situation was funny to them. They were armed and they assumed that we were unarmed and helpless. They had to know we were uneasy or even very frightened. They had to have chuckled and joked when they had made their plan to step out of the bushes into the road in the darkness with rifles in hand to block our only way out.

They sat down only a couple of feet behind us and I had made up my mind what I would do. If they pointed the guns at John or me, if they said one wrong word, even jokingly, if they seemed to be threatening our lives I would open fire. I would spin around in my seat with both hands on the revolver I was holding and fire point blank into their heads and I would not quit shooting until the gun was empty.

I could also see this very vividly in my mind. If John sensed imminent danger, he would floor the gas as I told him and the men behind us would be caught off guard and off balance. Then, before they could raise their rifles to shoot us, I would stop both of them with shots between their eyes.

Slowly John pulled away and we started towards the county road. I couldn't and didn't let my guard down for even one second. It was too important. My life and John's could depend on my immediate action.

Nothing more was said after they told us which direction to go until we neared an old farmhouse. It was Wathen's old home place. I had worked for him when I was a teenager pulling weeds out of his soybean fields. That's where they were wanting to go. "The shop" as they called it was the barn where tools and a tractor were kept.

Finally, my nerves began to calm down some. Why didn't they explain themselves better? Evidently, they had done it on purpose to frighten us. If they had only known what I planned to do if they had said one wrong word, even as a joke or made one wrong move. If they only knew that one, wrong word could have cost them their lives. If they would have known this, I don't think it would have been so funny to them. We were not in real danger, but we believed we were. They, on the other hand, did not think they were in any danger at all, but really were.

If they would have only known how near they came to dying. If they knew I held a loaded, cocked gun on the ready in the darkness to end their lives they would not have thought it was a laughing matter.

Yes, if things would have gone another way the last thing they would have seen was a bright flash in the darkness from the fire issuing from the muzzle of a gun. They were very lucky I kept my cool.

Chapter 6

The Outdoor Sportsman

In this chapter, I will discuss the gun owners that use their guns to shoot trap, skeet, or to take game. Some people just have a gun to keep at home for self-defense; some carry one for the same purpose, and others use long guns to hunt with or to shoot on the range. Then there are some that do all of the above.

Every day, Americans and most of the world, drive their cars to and from work or some other place and must deal with all the traffic laws. Sportsmen on the other hand, have many more laws to deal with. Each game species has different rules and regulations when they are pursued. This varies, but often they are restricted to using a certain size or type of gun, the shell or cartridge that goes in it, even the type of bullet or shot.

In my state of Indiana, a wild turkey can only be hunted with a firearm that is a10, 12, 16, or 20-gauge shotgun, as no rifles are allowed. The shot in the shell must be between sizes 4 to 7 ½. Any shot smaller or larger is illegal. However, no choke constriction is stipulated. Therefore, a person can legally hunt a turkey with a cylinder bore twenty-gauge shotgun with a very light load of ¾ of an ounce of tiny 7 1/2 sized shot. However, if that same person used a 28-gauge shotgun with a full choke and a full ounce of shot of larger size, it would be illegal. There are many such things that the sportsman must deal with in trying to obey all the hunting and even fishing regulations.

Not many years ago, the law was that if you came across a field during your scouting and found game birds there and then came back ten days later to hunt them, you could be arrested and fined. Why, you may ask. If someone had thrown grain in the field to attract the birds up to ten days before you hunted there, you would be charged with hunting over a baited field. It did not matter if you knew or not that the field had been baited. This would be like a person stopping by a bank and because it had been robbed a week earlier, that person would be charged for attempted robbery, just because they stopped at the bank. This bait law was later modified. It is still illegal to hunt over a baited field, but you are not guilty unless you knew or should have known that the field was baited.

There are even more rules and regulations in hunting migratory game birds. The gun has to be no larger than a 10-gauge. It cannot hold more than three shells. In addition, waterfowl can only be hunted with non-toxic shot. You cannot shoot after sunset. Then there are all the bag limits for each species. All these laws, however, are necessary for keeping the waterfowl population at a sustainable level. Many of these rules and regulations were put in place because in the late 1800's and early 1900's, market hunters decimated many duck, goose, and shorebird populations. Therefore, the sportsmen welcomed these laws.

Game wardens, or as they are called today, conservation officers, were hired by the government to enforce all the rules to ensure that the game birds, animals and fish are taken legally. They are there to protect the game. However, there have been times that this has not been the case. Many years ago, there was a story about conservation officers that were trying to catch some hunters that were shooting more than the limit. If I remember right, the hunters were hunting snow geese in Texas. The game wardens were staked out a short distance away watching. When the hunters shot more than their limit, the officers, instead of arresting them, kept watching. After the men had killed dozens of geese over the limit, then the officers made an arrest. They could have stopped the men the second the first illegal goose was killed. They, however, wanted to be able to brag that they had caught these guys that killed dozens of geese over the limit and to brag about how much of a fine they had to pay. These "conservation" officers did not care about the animals they were there to protect, they only wanted to have a sensational story that they could report. In my book, these officers should have been just as guilty or more, than the offending hunters.

Just as there is in any sport, and just as there is anywhere, there are the good, the bad, and the ugly when it comes to people. Most hunters love the outdoors and respect the game they hunt and follow the rules. Some hunters are game hogs and take more game than is legal. Then there are some that are not sportsmen or even hunters, they just shoot animals for the sake of killing them and then let them lie. This, too, is illegal, even if you have a hunting license and shoot the animals legally. It is called wanton waste.

I recently wrote a book called *Thou Shall Not Kill*. In it, I talk about the right or wrong of killing animals, domestic and wild. I even mention Cecil the lion that has caused so much controversy.

There has also been a campaign for many years to make sportsmen look like mean, cruel, heartless barbarians. I remember even as a young man, in the 1960's, watching an old episode of Mr. Ed, the talking horse. There was a story line about his master going duck hunting with a friend. The friend took along an expensive shotgun while Mr. Ed's master had a rifle he called "Old Betsy". The first mistake the producers made was that it is illegal to use a rifle when hunting migratory game birds, including ducks. The horse secretly followed them because he did not want them to kill a poor, helpless duck. While he was there at the lake, the horse saw a little baby duck. Waterfowl seasons are in the fall and winter, long after the nesting season is over. Therefore, there would not be any baby ducks.

To stop this duck hunt, Mr. Ed puts catsup on himself and claims a "hunter" shot him. This upsets his master and the friend who thinks of guns and hunting as being evil so they throw their guns in the lake. It was supposed to be an entertaining show, but it had many lies that cast a dark shadow on the sportsmen that have done so much to protect the wildlife they pursue. It is popular in movies and on TV to make all hunters as the villains.

Then there are movies like Bambi (which I have never watched). There would not be any baby deer during deer season either.

When Cecil the lion was killed, there was worldwide outrage over the death of a predator that kills animals all the time, even endangered elephants. That same day that the lion was killed, thousands of unborn human babies were also killed and not one word was said about that. No, Cecil should not have been hunted and killed. If those responsible did something illegal, they should face the consequences. Unethical hunters give a bad name to all others that obey the laws and respect the animals they hunt.

What makes it worse is that people actually wanted to murder the man that killed the lion. They value human life much lower than that of an animal. If that lion had killed a child or someone else, would they still want it to roam free? Probably many would. I care more about nature and conservation than most. I have written about it for many years. I have also studied nature since I was a child. Theodore Roosevelt was a hunter and a conservationist. He helped create many of the national parks, including Yellow Stone.

Often the news media takes things out of context and twists it around to make a hunter look bad. I have even seen them take sound bites to make it appear that the person said something they shouldn't have. One, just the other day, was about a girl hunter and she was reading a death threat from someone that had threatened her life. The sound bite that the news media used was edited to make it appear that she was making the death threat to someone that didn't agree with her.

The people that have to make up lies and malign others so they appear righteous, just fuel the fire. This is another reason that gun owners do not trust. People that are against all hunting and think it is wrong to kill animals should be vegetarians and never use any animal products. If not, they are a hypocrite. Anytime meat is eaten, an animal must die. This is an unpleasant fact. I have raised many kinds of poultry and it is much harder to kill a domestic animal that you have raised and one that has depended on you for food and protection than a wild one you do not know.

Yes, there are many animals that should never be killed and I discuss this in my book *Thou Shall Not Kill*. However, any animal that is born must someday die the same as we do. A quick death from a gun is much easier than to die of disease, starvation or to be torn apart by a predator.

There are many hungry people in the world, even right here in America. Every year, hunters give away tons of venison (that is deer meat) to food banks. There is no sense in people going hungry while deer are dying of starvation because they have over populated. Over population of many species would soon happen if there were not hunters to kill the excess animals.

Many forget, or do not know, that many species, which are common now, were once almost gone. It was money the hunters paid, that brought many of them back for all to enjoy. I don't think many would want to shell out the money that hunters have paid and do pay if suddenly hunting was outlawed or the guns that they use.

Recently, too, there have been many bear, cougar and coyote attacks. Many places have restricted hunting and the animals have lost their fear of man. When this happens, the predator looks at a human as just an easy meal. I believe an anti-gun person would quickly change their mind if a grizzly bear was charging them or a loved one and they knew that it was going to soon tear them apart, peace by peace. I believe they would wish someone was there with the biggest gun there was to stop that attack.

Most of the people that want all hunting to stop, thinking that it is cruel, should look around. The shopping mall they go to, the building they work in, and the home they come to every evening, was once on land that was wildlife habitat. A "legal" hunter just kills the surplus birds or animals. As long as there are enough animals to reproduce, the population will never diminish. However, if the animals' habitat is destroyed, they have nowhere to find food, shelter or raise their young.

People need to get their priorities straight. They need not lie, as there are enough problems without making up new ones. It will take all concerned, working together, to solve any complicated problem, even gun control.

Chapter 7

Carrying a Concealed Weapon

Today, more and more people are carrying concealed guns. It is no wonder. Crime is rampant. When I was a child, you almost never heard of a murder anywhere in the state. Now, anytime you turn on the local news, there has been a murder close by. Some of these murders are not crimes of passion, but they were committed just out of meanness or hate.

Recently even churches have not been spared. In the small church that I attend, three men carry a concealed gun just in case some crazed person decides to make the world news.

When I was a young man, I had a gun permit, but I rarely carried a gun on my person. However, I did often keep one in my vehicle. Now, since I am older, I carry a concealed handgun nearly everywhere I go.

One man at church told me that carrying his probably saved his life more than once. In one instance, two men tried to take his car and do him harm. When he took out his handgun, they quickly changed their minds and hurriedly left the scene.

Another friend of mine was in the National Guard and had to leave home sometimes on the weekends. One particular time, when he was gone, his wife had a visitor. A man came to the door and said he was trying to sell something. When my friend's wife (who was very attractive), answered the door, she had been washing the dishes and brought the drying towel along.

After telling the man at the door that she was not interested, he would not leave and kept asking to come in so he could talk to her. The only thing between them was a screen door. Even after repeatedly telling the man no, he would not leave. She was then becoming frightened. Therefore, she removed the towel in her hand, revealing a loaded semi-auto pistol. The man soon changed his mind, leaped from the porch, jumped over a hedge in the yard and continued running down the street. If she had not had the gun, there is no telling what would have happened.

There have been thousands of times that a gun has saved lives instead of taking them. I have heard stories of elderly people using a gun to protect themselves in their home where intruders came in to rob and kill them.

Just recently, a man carrying a concealed gun saved lives when the attack happened in Chattanooga, Tennessee where the five soldiers were killed at the recruitment station. However, this man that used his gun to save the lives of the unarmed soldiers, had charges brought against him for having a legal gun in an area where they were banned! This is the very thing that gun owners are afraid of; people in authority that are so stupid that they end up punishing a hero instead of the criminal. They often pass laws that make the innocent a criminal and let the real criminal go free. This is another reason that gun owners do not trust the government to pass gun control laws.

Chapter 8

Laws and More Laws

When President Kennedy was assassinated, it was with a bolt-action military rifle (unless you believe some of the conspiracy theories). As soon as he was killed, there was an uproar because this kind of rifle and could be bought through the mail. Laws were soon passed and it became illegal to buy one this way. A person had to buy one from a dealer or from someone personally.

I remember well the day that President Kennedy was assassinated. I was in the seventh-grade. I was sitting at my desk, in the classroom, when our teacher, Mr. Orth, came into the room looking somber. He then told the class that the President had been shot. It shocked everyone of course.

After President Kennedy's assassination, his brother Bobby Kennedy was also killed. On his campaign trail, Bobby Kennedy had come to Boonville, Indiana, where I went to high school. I wanted to go see him, but I did not get to, and it was not long afterwards that he was shot and killed. Around this same time in history, Marin Luther King Jr. was also assassinated and it happened to be on my birthday.

This was about the time that more laws were passed that outlawed "Saturday night specials". These types of guns were mostly cheap revolvers that could be bought for about $15.00, which was about a day's pay back then.

By the time I was in the military, more laws had been passed restricting the sale of even ammunition. Any cartridge that could be fired in a handgun could not be purchased by anyone under twenty-one years old. This sounded good to those that had no idea what this meant.

The idea was to stop people from buying cartridges that would to fire in a revolver or pistol. An eighteen-year-old person could buy a .460 Weatherby magnum cartridge that has about 7500 foot-pounds of energy and would shoot through the body of an elephant. However, a twenty-year-old man that was in the army and laying his life on the line for his country could not buy a .22 caliber BB cap, which would barely go through a tin can.

As I said in the introduction, when I was in the military, where I shot machineguns, threw hand grenades and was training to shoot down military aircraft with million dollar missiles, I could not by a box of .22 caliber shorts or a BB cap.

The people that pass the laws have very little knowledge it seems when it comes to firearms. If a criminal wants to harm someone, they could take a rifle and cut off the barrel and stock to make a handgun. About all these laws do is to make it harder on the law-abiding citizen.

Because of all the idiotic laws passed by politicians so they can say they are doing something about a situation, we have just more red tape that the law-abiding person must deal with. It seems that everyone is trying to deal with symptoms, not the cause of the problem.

Laws are also changing constantly. Years ago, if a person had a license to carry a handgun, this meant that they had already had a background check. Therefore, if they wished to buy a new gun they could purchase it on the spot. Now, even if you have a license, they do a background check. At least it is better than having to wait a week to get a gun you wanted to buy.

Even today, in many states, if you have a license to carry a gun and want to go a few miles to a gun shop, but it happens to be in an adjoining state, you cannot buy a handgun there. You must have it sent to your state to another licensed dealer. This then will cost more money because you must pay not only the shipping for the gun, but also you will be charged by the dealer in your state for his trouble of filling out the paperwork. Besides all this, there is the money spent for gasoline going back and forth, the time and inconvenience. If there would be a national system where a background check could be done instantly, you would not have to go through all this nonsense when you were already there at the gun shop that has the handgun you wanted to buy. Today you must go through all this red tape just because gun control laws are so tangled and sometimes ridiculous. The thinking about handguns is that they can be concealed. At the same shop, I just mentioned, you could buy a long gun without all the red tape. They still do a background check, but if you wanted to be a criminal, you could just modify the long gun, making it small enough to conceal.

Here is another ironic fact. A muzzle-loading gun is not considered a "real gun". It is not considered a "firearm" and because it is not, it is not regulated as such; even though the muzzle-loading gun has been around for over six-hundred years and was the only type of firearm for about five-hundred of those years. It was the weapon used in our Revolutionary War and our Civil War. This type of personal weapon killed more Americans during the Civil War than any other war including World War II.

I suppose it is not considered a real firearm because it is a "primitive weapon." It also takes so much time to load and fire that it would not be much of a danger if someone wanted to harm others, as they would only have one shot.

There is another thing that many who are against guns do not stop and think about. If young men did not learn to shoot well and had to fight in a war, they would be at a disadvantage. When America was attacked in World War II, hundreds of thousands of armed men had to fight for the freedom of the world. If America had not done so, just think of how different the world would be today. It would be living in a nightmare. In the final World War that is coming, America will not be able to stop the madness.

Chapter 9

Give an Inch; Take a Mile

Here is where the fear comes in. This is why the NRA and most gun owners feel threatened, and for good reason. Anytime the government gets involved with anything they screw it up. It does not matter what the issue, when there are laws passed to stop one problem it crates ten more.

Every American can look around and see what I am talking about. Tax laws are passed to try to be fair and then someone will find "loopholes" and get away with paying very little or no taxes at all, then it causes the burden to be on others. Bureaucrats try to make it better for one section of the population so they crate laws against discrimination and then the new law discriminates against others.

We can learn a lesson when the federal government enacted Prohibition Laws and they were put into effect between 1920 to 1933. These laws made it a crime to manufacture, transport or sell any alcoholic drink in America. The thought was, "If there is no alcohol, then there would be no drunk drivers, no bar room brawls, no drunkards beating on their wives or drunks starting fights." It sounded good, but it caused one of the worse criminal periods in American history.

Why didn't it work? For one thing, it punished those that just enjoyed a little alcohol and did not abuse it. Then, because there were no legal sales of alcohol, some saw that they could make a lot of money selling it illegally. Crime skyrocketed and there were murders and robberies everywhere. Anyone that has seen an old movie about the "roaring twenties" knows how men with machineguns ruled as crime bosses in some of the big US cities.

It was also during this time, that many of the gun laws were passed that we have today. Machineguns were outlawed. Short-barreled shotguns were part of the illegal guns that could not be possessed. There were also others, such as the pistols that could not have a smoothbore barrel.

Many cities have restrictive gun laws and it has not stopped crime, it has risen. Some might say it is because they can get the guns from a neighboring state. This is true, but who is getting them? Criminals are the ones that buy them to commit crime and they are not buying them legally. Most are stolen. In some countries, if a gun is stolen and a crime is committed with it, the gun owner is held responsible! Can you imagine the outcry if your car was stolen and the person that took it ran over someone and killed them or used your car to rob a bank and you were charged with the crime! No one would stand for that, yet there have been laws passed that do just that when it comes to gun owners. Why? It is because there are some that view a gun as "bad" and do not want anyone to have one. This is one reason many Americans are afraid of what those that want to pass "gun control" laws will do if they have their way.

"We don't want to take away all the guns," some will say. "We just want to ban the bad ones; the ones like assault weapons." Okay, this is where we are right now. This is the reason for this book and this chapter. What is an "assault weapon"? Many will say, "It is those guns that look like what the army or police have in fighting war or crime. It is those "automatic guns" that shoot dozens or rounds". Now we are getting to the issue we face in America today. "Automatic guns" as many call them, are not "automatic weapons" they are semi-automatic guns. What is an "assault weapon," or for that matter a "weapon"? A weapon is a gun that is used to kill. A knife can also be a weapon, as can a sword, a hatchet, an ax, a baseball bat, a bomb, a stick, or a rock. It is anything that is used to kill or injure someone. Until it is used as a weapon, it is not a weapon, it is what it is.

"You know what I mean, it is one of those guns that looks scary and can kill a lot of people." Any gun looks scary to some people. Some people are terrified of snakes. It does not matter if they are harmless or not. Just to see one scares them to death. I had a neighbor lady like that and my mother was not too fond of them either. Once you know which snakes are harmless and become familiar with them your fear lessens or goes away.

If you remember in an earlier chapter, I mentioned the different types of guns. These "assault weapons" only look different on the outside. The mechanisms inside are the same as many other guns. There are many sporting arms that work on the same principal and automatically feed the next round into the chamber of the gun after each shot is fired. This is why many call them automatics. As said earlier, no American citizen can legally own or possess a fully automatic gun without a special license. The only real difference between these "assault weapons" as many call them and any other sporting gun is the kind of stock that is on them. Many sporting guns can be fitted with different stocks and in some places, these are even illegal. Why? It is the same gun, but it looks different. Because it looks different, even though it is the same gun, people want to ban them. The stock does not even have to look "military" only a little different. I know because I bought a beautiful thumbhole stock for one of my guns and they are illegal in some states. The stock is not much different from the one on the gun, except it has a hole in the stock so you can insert your thumb; thereby holding it steadier as you aim at your target. This is ridiculous to restrict or ban a wooden stock just because of slight variations in its look. This is one reason people are up in arms over the government getting involved with passing gun laws. Most politicians do not know one gun from another.

There are also many horror stories about legal gun owners or guns shops being targeted by the ATF; many times, breaking the laws themselves. I believe most can remember the "sting operation" where "illegal guns" *were allowed to be bought* and later they ended up killing a law enforcement officer and others.

This is just one of the many fears that gun owner has. If the wording of the laws is not written well or some judge thinks that he knows what it "really means," then guns with the same "mechanical mechanism" could be outlawed. This could mean any gun that can self-load the next round. This would cover all auto-loading pistols, many hunting rifles, and many shotguns. The next step would be to limit the number of rounds the gun can hold. There are already people trying to limit the number of rounds a gun can hold at one time. I do not care to have a gun that can shoot a hundred rounds without reloading. On the other hand, I don't go to an outdoor range where I could shoot that many. What would be a "safe" number of rounds a gun should hold? I have clips for some guns that hold, five, ten and twenty. These are the norm. Some tube fed rifles hold from ten or so to over twenty; it is just according to what caliber and what make of gun. A tubular fed .22 rimfire rifle can hold up to 22 rounds, while a lever action, big bore rifle, can only hold a handful.

You can see that it gets complicated and I have only scratched the surface. Where do you draw the line? If someone does not have a giant clip that can hold one-hundred rounds, they can have five that holds twenty rounds or ten that holds ten rounds. Should we then limit how many clips a person can have? What about limiting the number of rounds a person can buy in a week, in a month, or in a year?

This war on gun owners is relentless. Every time people are killed and it makes national news, there is more outrage and there is a call for more and tougher gun control laws to be passed. I understand that no one wants his or her loved ones shot and killed. I also do not want them to be killed by a drunk driver, robbed, beaten or raped.

A good analogy about the issue of gun control would be if someone has a fire burning in a stove to keep the house warm. A person in the house has a great fear that the fire could burn the house down, thus killing them. Therefore, they want to put it out. They think that if there is no fire, they will be safe. Once the fire is out, however, they freeze to death. The moral of the story is that guns can kill just as a fire can, but guns can also save lives, just as a fire can. It is according to how it is used.

I agree that many people should not be allowed to own a gun. Criminals that have shown a tendency to be violent or have been violent should not own one. The problem is that a criminal does not care if they break the law; that is why he or she is called a criminal. There are many laws on the books that try to stop criminals from obtaining a gun, but if someone wants to get one bad enough they will do so. On the other hand, if they cannot get a gun, they can use another weapon. Many attacks, even in recent memory, have been with hatchets, hammers, machetes, knives, even bombs. If we ban all guns, then we will have to ban all the other things that could be used as weapons. Many will say, "We just want the guns off the streets. Let's first get the "assault weapons" banned. Later, we can outlaw guns that hold a lot of bullets. People do not need repeating guns either so let's get rid of those. Yes, first, we will outlaw these really bad guns, then we will get rid of handguns because they kill a lot of people, too. After this, we can work on getting shotguns and rifles taken away from everyone. Then the world will be much better and safer. We can then all live in peace and harmony."

Now we have hit the real problem. This is exactly why there is so much resistance to having gun control. I believe all Americans believe that mentally unstable people should not be allowed to have a gun; a gun they can use to hurt people with. However, if these same people want to hurt others they will use bombs, some other device or even a car. A bomb, more than likely, would kill a higher number of people than a gun. There are already laws on the books that make it illegal to buy a gun if the person is mental unstable. The states should get together and have a system that very quickly can conduct a background check. In my state of Indiana, you must fill out a form to purchase a new gun. As you are doing so, the retailer calls and does a background check while you are waiting. If you have a record of committing a crime that disallows you from buying a firearm, you will not be allowed to purchase it.

There is a push for registering all guns and this is another thing that frightens gun owners. Almost no one would care if their guns were registered, because if stolen and found they could be returned to the rightful owner. The fear is, that the once all the guns are registered, it is just one step closer to the government seizing them.

Many, if not most people in America, do not trust their government. The reason being is that they can look back at history and see what has happened. There were treaties made with Native Americans and nearly everyone was broken because "conditions changed". Japanese-American citizens were rounded up and put into internment camps at the onset of World War II. American Eskimos were ordered to leave their homes is Alaska so the military could station defenses there during World War II and they were never given their homes back. I could go on and on with dozens of examples of how the government has said one thing then done another. This was why there was the Constitution and the Amendments added to it. They were to guarantee that the rights of the people would not be taken away. The founding fathers knew how government worked. Our country was founded because of religious persecution in the mother country. The king of England had suppressed his citizens and did things that were unfair. The Constitution was written to try to keep those things from happening here. However, the persecution of people of faith has already begun again. They are being forced to go against their beliefs if their beliefs are not "politically correct."

Today, a few judges can overrule millions of Americans. Four or five people can make a decision that causes untold suffering and pain. In 1857, in the Dread-Scott decision, the Supreme Court said that any black person in America was not a citizen and that slaves were the property of the slave owners. This meant that the slave could be sold, beaten, whipped, tortured, raped or killed and it was up to the owner to decide how they were to be treated. They said that blacks were not real human beings and that they were property. This one decision finally lead to the Civil War and over 600,000 thousand Americans dying, not counting all the maimed and wounded. In 1973, the Supreme Court ruled that a fetus is not a real human being and that it is the property of the mother and can be killed during the first three months in the womb. Later, the time line was moved up and the babies could be killed during the second trimester. Soon the babies, as they were being born, were killed because it was said that it was "legal" for they were not completely out of the womb. You can now see how a decision of a few people can cause great and dire consequences. You can also see if one law is passed how it is soon changed and more and more freedoms are taken away. It is like the analogy of a frog in hot water. If the water temperature is turned up just a little at a time, the poor frog does not realize what is happing until it is too late and he dies.

Chapter 10

What if there were no guns?

Some think that if guns were unavailable the world would be a lot less dangerous. Therefore, let's examine that scenario.

If tomorrow all guns were outlawed and no American citizen could own or possess one for any reason, what would happen? No law official would have one either, because they could be stolen, or the cop could use it on an innocent person. You would also have to take all the guns away from the military because they, too, could be stolen and used in crime. Then you would have to get the entire world to stop making them and destroy everyone that already exists. You are thinking that can't be done, we have to have the military to protect us! Okay let's give the guns just to the military. What about the police? Should just state police have them or local police as well? Should the sheriff's department have guns? What about the FBI, CIA, or the Secret Service personnel that protects the President?

"No, we just want the average person not to have a gun. They don't need one, they have the police to protect them. Their guns can be stolen and used in crime. People today do not need a gun any longer. It would also stop the killing of animals because hunting hurts animals. People do not need to hunt; they can go to the supermarket to buy meat if they want."

Okay, we have just disarmed every citizen in America. Here are some of the things that people say and believe: "You can go to bed tonight in peace and safety. Your kids can go to school and not worry about being killed. You can go to a movie and not worry about being shot. You can even walk alone at night on a dark, lonely street and be safe. Your kids, too, can walk home from school or play on the playground and never have to worry about being kidnaped. "Wait!" you say. Taking all guns away will not stop criminals from hurting me or from kidnapping my child. You are right. Actually, if the right person was there and had a gun it could very well stop the criminals from killing you or kidnapping your child.

Taking the guns away from everyone would stop a lot of crime; right? It would stop crime in a few cases. On the other hand, it would cause many more. If every person turned in their gun and all guns were outlawed, no one would have them; right? Wrong, very wrong! If guns were outlawed, then the outlaws would break the law and get them and of course, they would never turn them in. Criminals do not care about gun laws; they would buy them somewhere or even make them. If guns were not available, there would soon be a black market and those that made or stole them would become wealthy. When this happened, then those that did not have a gun would be at the mercy of the criminals. The world is full of crime now. If criminals knew that every citizen would be helpless, what would stop them from breaking in, stealing everything you own, raping and murdering anyone they wished? The only thing a criminal understands is force. If crime escalated, which it would, soon the unarmed citizen would become so frightened that they would break the law and try and steal or buy a gun on the black market also. Others would not turn in their guns because they would be afraid of what might happen to them. Now, tens if not hundreds of thousands of scared people are criminals, just because they wanted to protect themselves and their families.

In addition, if guns were made illegal and the crime rate stayed the same or became worse; what would be next? Bow and arrows would also have to be outlawed because people would resort to using those. Next on the list would be knifes, machetes, hatchets, axes, and chainsaws. The authorities would then have to stop all sales of any products that could be used in making a bomb, creating a chemical weapon or concocting some poisonous substance. No pressure cookers would be allowed, no kinds of metal pipes, no explosive chemicals, no propane or even gasoline. All vehicles would also have to be illegal because people could use them to kill as well as aircraft. You can see how crazy the world would be. You have to draw a line somewhere.

The problem is not with the objects that can be used as weapons, it is the people that use the objects as weapons. When my son was shot, I did not blame the gun, it was the fault of the person that left it loaded in the reach of a child. When the first recorded murder took place, there were no guns; there were no bow and arrows, and there were no swords. Cain killed his brother Abel with what was most likely a rock. When God confronted Cain for the murder, He did not say all rocks will be illegal to own or possess because they can be used as a weapon. He put the blame on the one responsible. The murder came from Cain's heart. This is where the heart of the problem lies. It is in the hearts of people.

Chapter 11

What Steps Should be Taken?

There should be a few steps taken that would protect the law-abiding gun owner and stop the criminal. I believe the Second Amendment itself should be reworded so it is very clear that every American citizen (unless they have a mental problem or a criminal record), can own a firearm for self-defense or recreational use. Moreover, that they can also carry a concealed gun if so desired for personal protection anywhere with just a few exceptions where it could be dangerous, such as on aircraft. I do not believe that loaded long guns should be carried in public unless there is some threat either locally or from the outside, such as terrorists. The gun owners need to respect others as well as wanting to be respected. I have a permit to carry a handgun openly, but I almost never do. I don't because I do not wish to alarm anyone. In addition, if a criminal that is bent on shooting people can see that a person is armed they will know who to shoot first.

I think, however, that it should be made clear, that *anyone* that is not an American citizen cannot own or possess a firearm without a temporary license that would stipulate the reason or reasons.

Some reasons could be firearms competition or hunting. I believe this is already the law, but evidently, it is not enforced in many cases. If an illegal alien is caught possessing a firearm or any *other weapon*, they should be deported immediately if that is their only crime. There also needs to be an agreement made with the country in which the person came, that they will not allow that person back in our country. If they do so, then the offending country will have to pay a substantial fine, the fine being the cost of keeping that criminal in our prisons for life. Otherwise, that country will have to keep the offending person in their prison system.

All laws should be looked at and changed if necessary so they are fair and consistent across the entire county. If someone robs a bank, that person can spend more time in prison than if someone murders another human being.

Lawsuits have also been filed against gun manufactures saying they should be held responsible for gun deaths, because guns can kill. These kinds of lawsuits just make the gun owners more afraid that their guns will be taken away and it causes more determination to fight any kind of gun laws. Therefore, the intended outcome is the opposite of what the lawsuit tried to do.

If there was a strengthened Second Amendment, then maybe gun owners would not be so afraid to register their guns. I do agree that all gun sales should be tracked, even private sales. This way, if the gun is used in a crime later, it will be known who had it last. However, when the government gets involved, they most likely would create so much red tape that it would probably end up costing the gun owner more to sell the gun than what it is worth. This is the way nearly all local, state or federal laws end up.

So, what is the answer? You cannot do away with laws; many people would do anything and everything they could if they knew they would get away with it. There should be laws and tough ones for those that commit crimes with a gun or any weapon.

In the following chapters, I will give the real reasons that there is a fight about gun control. It may surprise both gun owners and those that want guns to be banned.

Chapter 12

What will Happen in the Future?

Many will say that no one knows what will happen in the future. They would also be very wrong, however. You can look at history, see what has happened in the past and predict the future.

In the not too distant future, guns will be outlawed and those that think this will solve the problems will be in for a rude awakening. Guns will be outlawed because some will wish to impose their will and values on everyone else. You can already see it in the world today. Those with their own set of "moral values" who think their way is right will label all other people as criminals because they have a different set of values. When bad things happen, people need to blame someone. Today it is the gun owners.

This happened in Germany just before World War II. When the economy got bad, the Jews were blamed. If many of the six-million Jews, which were slaughtered during the time of Hitler's nightmarish regime, would have been armed, things may have been different. However, they, like sheep, were herded into trains where they were taken to camps to die. In World War II, is was American planes that dropped tens of thousands of tiny, cheaply made pistols called "Liberators" behind enemy lines. They did this to help the resistance.

The events, which took place during World War II, are reasons that frighten many Americans that own guns. Any study of history will show that events can quickly spiral out of control and a country and its citizens can suddenly find themselves in a nightmare scenario. This is why there are survivalist groups in many places across the country. They are afraid of what could happen or will happen in the future. Therefore, they stockpile, food, and other supplies along with guns and ammunition just in case of a natural or manmade disaster. They want to be prepared.

There is nothing wrong with being prepared for disasters because we never know when one may strike. However, counting on surviving "the end of the world" will not save you in the end.

I will be very blunt and what I am going to say may surprise many. Others, however, will know that I am telling the truth. In my view, most gun owners are more self-reliant and because of this, their faith may be stronger. I believe many of them get this from their ancestors that fled persecution, came to America and carved out a life in the harsh wilderness.

As I see it, America has only two choices. One choice is to go the way it has been going. The second choice is to turn around and go the opposite way. You might say, "What does that mean?" If America stays on the course it is on and the chances are very good that it will, soon our country will reap even more of what it has been sowing. It already has been reaping the seeds of destruction; that is another reason I wrote this book. This is why crime, terrorism, mass shootings and other terrible things happen every day. Many think it is because of guns. It is because of the people who use them and what is in their hearts.

If America does not return to the biblical faith, it once had, and stop pushing the Creator of the universe out of their lives, then this is what will happen. Crime will continue to escalate. Guns will be blamed more and more for the violence. Soon terrorism will become worse and worse as will the economy of the world. The stage will then be set for the leader of a one-world government to make his appearance. He will take away all guns from anyone that does not follow him and his policies, even if anyone has a gun by that time.

Those that have been stockpiling food, guns, ammunition and trying to get prepared for "the end" will not in the long run find that it will save them. Why? Of course, it helps to have provisions put back in case of an emergency and if the emergency does not last long, it can save you. However, when the end finally comes and the world gets bad enough as many survivalists think it could, their stockpiles will not save them. This is because during this time, if you ran out of food or any other items, you would not be able to buy any without the approval of the leader of the one-world government.

If you did have great stock piles of food and others were starving or desperate enough, you would be a target. You would soon be overrun with masses of people that would rather die from being shot than to starve to death. You would either, run out of bullets, get exhausted fighting and killing, or be overrun by hordes of people. Then all your supplies would be taken, and most likely, afterwards, you, too, would be killed.

Chapter 13

The Answer

The question at the beginning of this book was, "What is the answer?" Therefore, here it is.

I will not say what people may want to hear, I will tell the truth about what is really going on. Most do not realize that we are not just fighting a battle about guns; we are fighting a much bigger battle. We are fighting an unseen battle that is in the hearts and minds of people. It is because of what is in the hearts of men, that we will always need ways of protecting one's self and our loved ones from the evil in the world.

A gun is a tool, just as any other. It can be used for good or evil. Because of the evil in people's hearts, the entire world will continue to suffer. This will continue until man comes to the brink of destroying all life from the face of the earth. When this happens, God will then have to intervene and stop the madness once and for all.

Our country and the entire world, has strayed so far away from the moral values that we should have, that many do not even know what is right or wrong any longer. America has pushed God from our schools. We have taught the lie of evolution. We have killed countless millions of babies by abortion. We do not follow the original Ten Commandments we were given. Marriage is a holy union created by God himself, but now many have forsaken this truth for a lie. People of faith are not being allowed to express their beliefs. If you do not believe me, just say something that is not "politically correct" and see the reaction of people. If you stand up for moral values, you are labeled a "hatemonger". As I write this, a woman in Kentucky was just arrested and put in jail for her belief that homosexual marriage was wrong and because she would not issue a marriage license. She was told that she would be kept in jail until she changed her mind. This is the same thing that happened in ancient times to the Hebrew children that were thrown in the fiery furnace or Daniel being put in the lion's den. They would not deny their faith and do what the "law of the land" said. They believed that God's law superseded man's law and they were punished for it. This woman could stay in jail the rest for eighteen months; eighteen months out of her life, and being away from her family, just because she believes what the Bible says. Then what will happen after she is released? Will she go back to jail again and again if she will not bow down to what the government says is "politically correct?" What she knows in her heart is wrong? This goes to show how the government can turn on its own people and not follow the Constitution. The Constitution says that the "government shall make NO LAW restricting the freedom of religion." The government, however, tramples on the Constitution all the time. Just a few years ago, if a homosexual person committed sodomy they went to jail for it was a crime. Now, if anyone believes that it is wrong, they are lambasted for "being behind the times" or being stupid. Soon it will be a crime to even say it is wrong and people may go to jail as this poor woman did, even though God himself has said that it is an abomination. This country is soon to reap what it has sown and when it does, God will not step in the bail us out this time.

Why is there so much crime? Why to people live in fear and want to protect themselves with guns? Because those that think they know what is morally right make up their own set of moral values and then try to shove them down the throats of others. They do not want to be offended, but they don't care how they offend the ones that don't agree with them. Where do people get any sense of morality? For centuries, it has come from the Bible and the Ten Commandments. Laws against stealing, murder, rape, incest, lying and others were instituted because God gave these laws so people could live together in peace and harmony. Today, people do not want to hear what God thinks because they know more than He does. They will reap what they have sown because God is not mocked. He will give this country and the world what they ask for, but it will not be pretty.

When crime comes knocking on their door they will have no one to blame but they themselves. If they can make up their own set of moral values, then so can everyone else. The Lord himself said that just before He returns that there will be evil and violence all over the world as it was just before the flood in the days of Noah. We are getting there more and more each day.

The reason for this is that most of the world thinks it no longer needs God. Some countries see the western world as causing the moral decay of others. Much of this is true. Then we wonder why there is so much crime, why kids kill kids; why there are mass shootings or why terrorists try to kill us. We are reaping what we have sowed. No, no one has the right to kill innocent people for what others have done as has happened when some countries perceive that America is evil. However, we also do not have the right to do many of the things that we have done. No one it seems knows right from wrong any longer. Evil begets evil.

Is there anything we can do to stop what is happening? The world is caught in a trap and will be held in it until the armies of the world meet at Armageddon. We need to do our best to change the world, but more importantly, we need to change our own hearts.

Yes, there will be a day, and it will be in the not too distant future, that all guns will be done away with; not only guns, but also all weapons of war. All bombs, tanks, missiles, battleships and anything used to kill or destroy will be a thing of the past. There will not be any murder or any war ever again. There will be no hunting, no killing of animals, even for food. Even the predators on earth will cease killing their prey. How do I know this? The answers are right in the pages of your Bible.

Here are some verses from the Holy Bible that promises this: Isa 2:4-5: "And He shall judge among the nations, and shall rebuke many people: and they shall beat their swords into plowshares, and their spears into pruning hooks: nation shall not lift up sword against nation, neither shall they learn war anymore."

Isa 11:6-10 "The wolf also shall dwell with the lamb, and the leopard shall lie down with the young goat; and the steer and the young lion and the calf together; and a little child shall lead them. And the cow and the bear shall feed; their young ones shall lie down together: and the lion shall eat straw like the ox. And the nursing child shall play on the hole of the asp, and the weaned child shall put his hand on the scorpion's den. They shall not hurt nor destroy in all my holy mountain: for the earth shall be full of the knowledge of the LORD, as the waters cover the sea."

As I said, this will not happen until man has nearly destroyed all life from the earth. The Scriptures are in Mathew 24, Luke 21 and Mark 13. If you wish to know more, I have written a book called *Mysteries of the Bible.* There are dozens of prophecies that explain how and when these things are to take place. Most do not know or understand what is to unfold because they have not been told or have been given the wrong information.

Therefore, until that day when peace finally arrives, we will have to live on this earth with ever-increasing violence. Instead of focusing so much on gun control, we need to focus on controlling the evil in our world and in our own lives.

Chapter 14

In Summary

For the past few years, I have been writing for a regional outdoor magazine and early next year I will probably close up my laptop and cease writing outdoor articles. I have tried to write books and articles that can make a difference in the world. I will be leaving this life in the not too distant future and I want to leave it better than when I first arrived. I know, however, that it will not be so. I feel sorry for those that will be left behind because I know what lies ahead. Each of us needs to try to do his or her best while we dwell of the speck of dust in the universe. Our lives are so short and life quickly passes us by. One day you are a child laughing and playing on your father's knee. The next day, you are graduating school, getting married and raising kids of your own. Before you know it, you are old and feeble.

I have tried to write about topics that divide us. In doing so, I hoped to cause those that read my work to stop and think why they believe what they do. In the end, we will not have to answer to anyone but God. He will judge how we did with what we were given. "To whom much is given, much is required." This also applies to an entire nation. Abraham Lincoln quoted the Bible once when he said, "A house divided cannot stand." Our country was divided while he was president as never before, and he knew it could not last long if it stayed that way. This was why, even though it cost hundreds of thousands of American lives, he needed to preserve the union. Lincoln often went to the Bible to find the answers he needed and to give him strength. I have always admired him and counted myself privileged to have been born on the banks of Little Pigeon Creek just downstream from where he grew up.

I originally had many Bible Scriptures in this book to explain how things will unfold, which will lead to a one-world government and how guns could be taken away. I also explained how we could change the path we are on and turn America around and escape many of the things that lie ahead. I took the Scriptures out because many today do not want to hear them. I do have those in my book *Mysteries of the Bible* if you care to read it.

Our world is filled with hate and violence. It is also filled with love and compassion. I know which one will finally win out, but the battle will be great and the cost very high. Gun control is just the latest issue that I have written about. When I see a gun, I look at its beauty. I love the grain of a fine wood stock and the lines of a finely crafted piece of work. Many of the guns today are not beautiful and they are looking more like tools that are used to kill. Plastic has replaced the warm wood and laser sights have replaced the traditional ones. This is another reason that they frighten people. It is difficult enough if people do not understand that a gun can be used for good or evil, but when they look at the ones that are used just for killing humans it scares them. I can understand some of what they mean. Gun owners also need to try to put themselves in others' shoes. Both sides need to try to understand the other. It takes two to make a good marriage.

Yes, some just see a gun as a tool, or even a work of art. Some see them as weapon, or something they can use in a crime. Others see them as a thing to be feared, an evil invention and something they wish was done away with. Everyone perceives the world a little differently. The difference is what is in the heart. One of my proverbs I wrote says, "Love does not see the filth that covers a man, but hate sees the smallest speck on his garment."

I know my books will not touch many, but I also know some of the words I have written have changed lives and on at least one occasion saved a life. Even if you did not like much of what I had to say in this book, I hope that there may have been a few words that gave you more understanding. If you enjoyed this book, please read some of my others. In addition, even if you did not like this book, I have many others that you may enjoy. I have enjoyed writing stories that touch the heart and I like stories that make the reader laugh. This book has neither, but I felt it should be written.

I also have written several children's books and stories. As a substitute teacher, I loved to share my knowledge, love of animals and nature with the kids. I could see in their eyes the enthusiasm when I talked with them.

Yes, gun control is a controversial topic, but the only way to solve a problem is it to look at it and look for solutions. In this case, they are not easy. It seems the ones in authority want to do everything to fix the problem, except to take the correct steps to solve it.

As I was writing this book, there was a news story of two men that broke into a house, raped, tortured and killed three women. They also beat the husband nearly to death with a baseball bat. When they set the house on fire, the husband managed to escape. The barbarians that committed these crimes did not use a gun, but a gun would have prevented the atrocities and those three women would be alive now and there is a good chance the criminals would not. The criminals were caught and sentenced to death, but then the state "changed the law". Therefore, they will not have to die for what they did. A judge said, "Civilized societies should not impose the death penalty." The death penalty is the only thing that these criminals understand. If people knew that life was so precious that they would have to forfeit their own life for taking someone else's, then they might stop and think. These judges, too, that let violent criminals back on the street because of some technicality, when they know they are guilty, and that criminal commits another crime, should be held responsible for that crime. This would stop many of the idiotic decisions made by moronic judges.

"Thou shall not kill" really means "Thou shall not murder." Murder is the taking of an "innocent life". Taking the life of a murderer is called justice. These crimes happen because people call evil good and good evil. They have turned things around until they are backwards.

Instead of more laws for gun control, we should pass some laws that hold people responsible for what they do. This would go a long way in stopping crime.

I co-authored a book called *Madam President* with author Veronica Fox. The first woman president wins with the new Constitutional Party. The country becomes fed up with all the bickering and strife of the two parties and she wins by a landslide. After an assassination attempt, she is the first modern president to carry a gun.

If you think Donald Trump is outspoken, Madam President makes him look like a shy little school boy, although she does have a lot more wit and charm. She is very outspoken about gun control, abortion, gay marriage and corruption by those in authority. She also has female bodyguards: Sherry, Marilyn and "Thunder". It is a 93,000-word novel and I think people will enjoy it. If you liked this book at all, I believe you would love that one.

Remember to view things in perspective. We may not be able to change the world, but we can give it our best shot.

"The earth is but a grain of sand on the beach where God walks."—Kenneth Edward Barnes

About the Author

Kenneth Edward Barnes has been called, *"A modern day Mark Twain"* by a local newspaper reporter. *"He shows a Twain sense of humor in conversation and in his writing. He writes in the 'down to earth' style that Twain used to capture the heart of America."*

He was born on April 4, 1951, along the banks of Little Pigeon Creek in the southern tip of Indiana, downstream from where Abraham Lincoln grew up. As a child, he loved fishing from the muddy banks of the creek and roaming in the nearby woods. He never missed an opportunity to be in the outdoors where he could see all of God's creation.

Ken is a nationally published writer, poet and the author of over seventy-five books. Some of his most popular ones are: *A Cabin in the Woods; Mysteries of the Bible; Madam President; Life Along Little Pigeon Creek; A Children's Story Collection; Buddy and Rambo: The Orphaned Raccoons; The Golden Sparrow; My Favorite Poems; Betrayed; The Arkansas River Monster; The Coming Invasion; Barnestorming the Outdoors, and Do Pets go to Heaven?* This could soon change, however, as he has recently written several others.

The author became a member of *Hoosier Outdoor Writers* in 1993, where he has won several awards from them in their annual writing contest. He has also been a guest speaker for the *Boy Scouts, Daughters of the American Revolution, Teachers Reading Counsel, Kiwanis Club*, and at several schools, libraries and churches.

Ken has been an outdoor columnist and contributing editor for several newspapers and magazines: *Ohio Valley Sportsman, Kentucky Woods and Waters, Southern Indiana Outdoors, Fur-Fish-Game, Wild Outdoor World, Mid-West Outdoors,* and a hard cover book titled *From the Field.* He has written for the *Boonville Standard, Perry County News, Newburgh Register and Chandler Post.* He has had poems published locally and nationally. One titled *The Stranger* went to missionaries around the world. The poem, *Princess,* was also published locally and nationally, and won honorable mention in a national contest. His best-loved poem is *Condemned,* and has been published by the tens of thousands. Nearly every single poem he has written is in his colored paperback book, *Poems from the Heart* and the e-book *My Favorite Poems.*

Ken has worked for an Evansville, Indiana, television station where he had outdoor news segments aired that he wrote, directed and edited. He also had film clips that were aired on the national television shows *Real TV* and *Animal Planet.* At this time, he has several short videos on YouTube and on GodTube.

Studying nature since childhood, he is a self-taught ornithologist and a conservationist. In 2009, he became founder and president of the *Golden Sparrow Nature Society*, the name of which was chosen because of his first published book. Ken loves to share his knowledge and love of nature, and it has been said that he is a walking encyclopedia on birds and animals. Because of this, he recently published an e-book titled *Birds and Animals of Southern Indiana.* It has over 300 photos of birds and animals, most of which he photographed himself. He frequently updates it with new photos.

He has followed his dream of being a writer since 1978 and now lives in a cabin in the woods. Being an individualist, he cleared the land, dug a well by hand and built the house himself, which uses only solar electric. He even wrote a book titled *Solar Electric: How does that work?*

Comments on the author's work can be left on his Facebook page at: **Kenneth Edward Barnes**, or on **Twitter** at **Kenneth Edward Barne @BarneKenneth.** Questions and comments to the author can also be left at the **Author's Page** on **Goodreads**. All of Ken's books can be seen on his **Author Page** at Amazon and at Goodreads.

Books by Kenneth Edward Barnes in:
Paperback, Hardcover and E-book

1. In Search of a Golden Sparrow
2. Life on Pigeon Creek
3. Barnestorming the Outdoors
4. Invasion of the Dregs
5. A Children's Story Collection
6. Poems from the Heart
7. The B.O.O.K. (Bible Of Observational Knowledge)
Under the pen name of ZTW

Books available as E-books only:

8. A Cabin in the Woods
9. Life Along Little Pigeon Creek (a newer longer version)
10. The Long Pond Road
11. The Golden Sparrow (a newer longer version)

61. The Adventures of Ralph and Fred
62. Twelve Tantalizing Tongue Twisting Tales
63. Kenneth Edward Barnes: An Autobiography
64. Kenny's Collection of Children's Stories
65. Children's Stories II
66. The Lost Land of Adreus
67. The Creature of O'Minee
68. Buddy and Rambo: The Orphan Raccoons
69. I Don't Want to be a Pig!
70. Buzz: The Cowfly
71. The Watermelon Turtle
72. The Eagle and the Hummingbird
73. The Grumbling Grasshopper
74. Who? What? When" Where" Why?
75. Buggies:
(Also, includes: Animal Cracks and other jokes and riddles)
76. Plays for Children